FAMOUS LIVES

The Story of
HARRIET TUBMAN
Conductor of the Underground Railroad

By Kate McMullan
Illustrated by Steven James Petruccio

Gareth Stevens Publishing
MILWAUKEE

Dedicated to Rain Loper

For a free color catalog describing Gareth Stevens Publishing's list of high-quality books and multimedia programs, call 1-800-542-2595 (USA) or 1-800-461-9120 (Canada). Gareth Stevens Publishing's Fax: (414) 225-0377.
See our catalog, too, on the World Wide Web: http://gsinc.com

Library of Congress Cataloging-in-Publication Data

McMullan, Kate.
    The story of Harriet Tubman: conductor of the underground
railroad / by Kate McMullan ; illustrated by Steven James Petruccio.
        p. cm. — (Famous lives)
    Includes index.
    Summary: A biography of the African-American woman who escaped
from slavery, led slaves to freedom on the Underground Railroad, aided
Northern troops during the Civil War, and worked for women's suffrage.
    ISBN 0-8368-1479-7 (lib. bdg.)
    1. Tubman, Harriet, 1821-1913—Juvenile literature. 2. Slaves—
United States—Biography—Juvenile literature. 3. African-Americans—
Biography—Juvenile literature. 4. Underground railroad—Juvenile
literature. 5. Antislavery movements—United States—Juvenile
literature. [1. Tubman, Harriet, 1821-1913. 2. Slaves. 3. African-
Americans—Biography. 4. Women—Biography. 5. Underground
railroad.] I. Petruccio, Steven, ill. II. Title. III. Series: Famous lives
(Milwaukee, Wis.).
E444.T82M38   1997
305.5'67'092—dc20
[B]   96-30710

The events described in this book are true. They have been carefully researched and excerpted from authentic biographies, writings, and commentaries. No part of this biography has been fictionalized. To learn more about Harriet Tubman, refer to the list of books and videos at the back of this book or ask your librarian to recommend other fine books and videos.

This edition first published in 1997 by
Gareth Stevens Publishing
1555 North RiverCenter Drive, Suite 201
Milwaukee, Wisconsin 53212 USA

Original © 1991 by Parachute Press, Inc. as a Yearling Biography. Illustrations © 1991 Steven James Petruccio. Published by arrangement with Bantam Doubleday Dell Books for Young Readers, a division of Bantam Doubleday Dell Publishing Group, Inc. Additional end matter © 1997 by Gareth Stevens, Inc.

The trademark Yearling® is registered in the U.S. Patent and Trademark Office.
The trademark Dell® is registered in the U.S. Patent and Trademark Office.

Printed in the United States of America

1 2 3 4 5 6 7 8 9 01 00 99 98 97

Contents

STEVEN JAMES PETRUCCIO

Hired Out!

Two small black children drew with sticks in the dirt in front of a ramshackle cabin. Their older sister, Minty, whose real name was Harriet Ross, watched them. She wished that she could play, too. But she had work to do. It was a warm fall day. The field hands who picked crops for Edward Brodas would be thirsty. She must carry water to them. Minty picked up the heavy water buckets. She had no time for play.

It was 1827 in Dorchester County, Maryland, and Minty was six years old.

Dressed only in a scratchy, knee-length shirt, Minty carried the buckets past many log cabins. One of them was her home. Like all the others, it had only one small room. It had no windows. The roof sagged and leaked. The floor was hard-packed dirt. In the winter bitter

1

wind blew in through the cracks between the logs. Then Minty was glad to snuggle close to her nine brothers and sisters to keep warm.

From the road Minty could see the Big House. That was where the white folks lived. Though she was very young, life didn't seem fair to Minty. But when she complained, her parents, Ben and Rit, just shook their heads. That's how things are, they told her.

The Big House was enormous. Minty had never been inside to see its parlors, ballroom, bedrooms, or many guest rooms. In back of the Big House stood the cookhouse, where meals for the Brodas family were prepared. A little way off were the stables. The whole plantation belonged to Mr. Brodas.

Minty belonged to Mr. Brodas, too. He had a piece of paper that said she and her family were his property. Minty's mother worked in the Big House. Her father cut timber. They worked very hard. But they earned no money because they were slaves.

Today Minty noticed a wagon parked beside the Big House. She saw the front door of the Big House open. A woman came out with Mr. Brodas. The woman climbed up onto the wagon seat. Mr. Brodas mounted his horse. He rode toward Minty.

Mr. Brodas knew that Minty was a good worker. He knew how she carried heavy buckets so that his field slaves would have water to drink. He knew how she helped her parents when they came home tired at the end of the day. Before Minty realized what was happening, Mr. Brodas stopped his horse right in front of her. He picked her up and put her into the wagon. Mr. Brodas told her that she had been hired out. This strange white woman, Mrs. James Cook, was her mistress now. Mrs. Cook would pay Mr. Brodas for Minty's work.

Mrs. Cook slapped her horse with the reins. Off the wagon went, carrying Minty away from her home. Tears sprang to Minty's eyes. Her heart beat with fear. She had no idea where Mrs. Cook lived. Would she ever see her family again?

Terrified, Minty remembered how her two older sisters had been taken away, crying and screaming. They weren't much more than six or seven years old at the time. A slave trader from the South came to the Big House. Mr. Brodas sold Minty's sisters to him. The slave

3

trader put chains around their ankles. Then he whipped them and forced them to begin walking South, chained together. Minty never saw her sisters again.

Back in the slave quarters, Rit learned that Minty had been hired out. With an aching heart, Rit found comfort in the fact that at least her daughter had not been sold.

Mrs. Cook's wagon traveled on and on, far from the Brodas plantation. Not until after sunset did it stop at a log house. It was far finer than a slave's cabin. It had several rooms and an upstairs. But it was nothing like the Big House. The Cooks were not as rich as Mr. Brodas.

Mrs. Cook opened the door to her cookshed. She told Harriet to go inside. She gave the little girl a piece of corn bread for her supper. Then Mrs. Cook pointed to a corner near the fireplace. She told Minty to sleep there. Mrs. Cook told her to be ready to work first thing in the morning.

Mrs. Cook left. Minty was alone in the dark shed. She crouched down in her corner, too miserable to eat. With no blanket and no brothers or sisters to keep her warm, Minty cried herself to sleep.

The next morning Mrs. Cook brought Minty into the log house. She showed her a big loom. Mrs. Cook used it to weave cloth. She had hired Minty to help her. Minty was to stand up all day, winding yarn into balls for Mrs. Cook.

It wasn't easy. The yarn had to be wound with just the right tightness. Over and over Mrs. Cook warned her to be careful.

Minty tried her best to do what Mrs. Cook wanted. But the yarn tangled in her fingers. Lint from the yarn rose in the air. It tickled Minty's nose and made her sneeze. Her eyes watered. But she wasn't allowed to stop. If she broke a piece of yarn, Mrs. Cook would lash her with a long, stinging whip.

At mealtimes the Cooks fed Minty scraps from their plates as if she were no better than a dog. At night they sent her to sleep in the cook-shed. Winter came, but the Cooks did not give Minty a blanket. When the cooking fire went out, she put her feet under the ashes to keep them warm.

Minty tried to do as she was told. But Mrs. Cook was not happy with her. She called her clumsy and slow. So Mr. Cook said Minty could help him. He was a muskrat trapper.

Mr. Cook had Minty wade barefoot in the river. He showed her how to set traps for muskrats. Even though she often shivered with cold, she preferred this work to weaving. It was hard, but at least she was outdoors. She liked to see the muskrats swimming in the wide, free-flowing river.

One day Minty woke up with a fever. She felt dizzy and sick. But Mr. Cook made her go out to set his traps. Wading in the icy water made Minty even sicker. She grew so sick that at last Rit heard about it from a slave who had been out to the Cooks' house. Rit went to Mr. Brodas. She asked him to let Minty come home so she could take care of her. Mr. Brodas didn't want one of his slaves to die. Slaves were worth money. So Minty was brought home.

How good it felt to be back in her mother's arms! Minty had had the measles. Wading in the river had given her bronchitis, too. But Rit knew how to make powerful medicines from herbs and roots. Under her loving care, Minty slowly got well.

As soon as she was healthy, Mr. Brodas hired her out to the Cooks again. Now she was to help only with the weaving. She couldn't go outside. She couldn't walk by the river. She felt as trapped as one of Mr. Cook's muskrats!

Minty hated the noise of the loom and the spinning wheel. She hated getting lint in her nose and eyes. So Minty decided that she would not learn to weave. She simply refused!

From that moment on, nothing that Mrs. Cook told her seemed to sink in. Her mistress called her stupid. She whipped her constantly. But it did no good. At last Mrs. Cook said she was the most thick-headed girl in the world. But Minty didn't mind, because thick-headed girls got sent home!

Miss Susan

Of course Rit and Ben were happy to have their seven-year-old daughter back with them again. But they were worried, too. Minty had not pleased her mistress. They knew that she had not tried hard to learn to weave. Slaves who didn't work hard were sold.

Rit and Ben also worried about the Brodas plantation. Once it had raised tobacco. It had been a rich plantation. Then the price of tobacco dropped. Mr. Brodas had tried raising wheat and corn, and then cotton. But nothing paid as well as tobacco had. The Brodas plantation was becoming run-down and seedy.

But there was one thing Mr. Brodas still raised profitably, and that was slaves. It pleased him that Rit and Ben now had eleven children. Each child that was born was worth money to Mr. Brodas. He raised slaves the way some ranchers raised cattle. When he needed money, he hired them out or sold them.

Rit and Ben lived in fear that Mr. Brodas would sell the rest of their children. It would break their hearts. But there was nothing they could do to stop him.

Rit grumbled that she should be free. When her old master had died, he left a will that said so. And if she was free, her children should be free. But in 1828 black people like Rit and Ben had no rights.

Before long Minty was hired out once more. Again a wagon took her far from her home. At last it stopped in front of a house. It was much finer than the Cook's cabin, but not so fine as the Brodas house.

The house belonged to Miss Susan and her husband. During the day Minty's job was to help Miss Susan and her visiting sister, Miss Emily, with the housework. At night she was to care for Miss Susan's baby.

The first morning Minty was told to sweep and dust the parlor. Minty had never seen such a fine room as that parlor. She didn't know how to begin sweeping the soft carpet or dusting so many tables and chairs. But she got a broom and swept the carpet as hard as she could. Dust swirled into the air. Then she got a cloth and dusted the furniture. But the dust from the carpet was still in the air. Slowly it settled on the newly dusted furniture.

Miss Susan came into the parlor. Minty watched as she ran her finger over a table. Her finger made a streak. The table was dusty.

Miss Susan yelled at Minty. She called her stupid. She told her to do it again, and to do it right!

Minty was frightened. She'd swept and dusted as she'd been told. She didn't know what she'd done wrong. Still, she tried again. But when she finished, Miss Susan still found dust on her table.

Miss Susan got her whip. She whipped Minty over and over again. The child screamed in pain.

"Susan! Susan!" Miss Emily's voice called over the screaming. "What are you doing?" She had heard Minty's cries and had come downstairs. "Why do you whip the child for not doing what she has never been taught to do?"

Miss Emily asked Miss Susan to leave Minty alone with her for a few minutes. Then she showed Minty how to sweep and dust the right way.

Minty spent her days cleaning. When she wasn't cleaning, Minty took care of Miss Susan's baby. Years later she remembered, "I was so little I had to sit on the floor and have the baby put in my lap. And that baby was always in my lap except when it was asleep or its mother was feeding it."

But Minty's nights were the worst. Miss Susan did not want to be disturbed by a crying baby. She wanted a good night's sleep. So Minty had to rock the cradle back and forth so the baby wouldn't cry. At last the baby would fall asleep. Then Minty could sleep, too, on the floor beside the cradle. But often the baby woke up crying in the middle of the night. Then Miss Susan would leap out of bed. But she did not run to comfort her baby. Instead, she grabbed the whip she kept on a little shelf close to her pillow. Angrily she would lash Minty. How dare she let that baby wake up her mistress!

Soon Minty hardly slept at night for fear that the baby might start crying. She became exhausted. Then she couldn't work well. And when she made a mistake, Miss Susan would thrash her with a whip. The back of Minty's neck became covered with scars that remained all her life.

11

STEVEN JAMES PETRUCCIO

Minty thought of running away from Miss Susan. But she was afraid. She had no idea where she was. How could she ever find the Brodas plantation? She would probably be caught. And she knew what would happen then. Slaves who tried to escape were whipped and branded like cattle with a big letter *R* for "runaway." Sometimes their masters cut parts of their ears off. And then the next time a trader came from the Deep South, the slave would be sold and sent away in chains.

One Friday morning, after breakfast, Miss Susan was holding the baby. Minty stood by the kitchen table, ready to take it from her. Miss Susan was quarreling with her husband. She scolded him and called him all sorts of names.

As Minty waited for the baby, she looked down at the kitchen table. Her eye caught a bowl full of sugar cubes. Minty had never tasted sugar in her life, but she knew from the way people talked about it that it must be good. Miss Susan's back was turned. She was screaming at her husband. Minty didn't think she'd notice if she took just one lump. But as she reached out toward the bowl, Miss Susan whirled around. She screeched at Minty and snatched up her whip!

Minty didn't stop to think. She simply flew out the door and ran! Miss Susan and her husband chased after her, but Minty ran too fast for them. She ran past many houses, but she didn't dare stop. Everyone in the area knew Miss Susan. They would just send Minty back.

At last Miss Susan and her husband stopped chasing Minty, but still she ran. Finally she was too tired to run any farther. She slowed down. After a while she came to a great big pigpen. An old sow lived there with about ten piglets. Minty managed to tumble over the fence and into the pen. She was so exhausted that she couldn't move.

Minty hid in the pigpen for five days. She fought with the piglets for the potato peels and other scraps that were thrown into the trough. But the mother sow would push her away. She wouldn't let Minty eat any of her little pigs' food. At last she was close to starving. She couldn't survive in the pigpen. She had nowhere else to go. So Minty went back to Miss Susan's.

Minty nearly died from the whipping Miss Susan gave her. Then Miss Susan shoved her into the wagon and took her back to Mr. Brodas. "This girl," she told him, "isn't worth a sixpence."

Once more Rit nursed her near-starving child. She washed off the dirt from the pigpen and put herbal medicines on the fresh whip marks on Minty's neck. Little by little Minty gained weight and became healthy again.

Minty Takes a Stand

Of course, once Minty was well, Mr. Brodas hired her out again. But he had given up on her as a household worker. Mr. Brodas hired her out as a field hand.

Rit shook her head when she heard this. Field work was thought to be the lowest work a slave could do. It was backbreaking labor— loading wood onto wagons, working a plow, driving oxen, and splitting rails. Yet Minty preferred it to tending Miss Susan's baby.

Field work gave her the chance to be outside. She watched the sky and learned to predict the weather. She got to know the swampland and the plants that grew there.

Work in the fields callused Minty's hands. Her muscles grew strong and hard. Although she was still a child, she did the work of a man. Soon she graduated from the scratchy linen

16

shirt to the long dress of a woman. When she worked in the field, she tucked her skirt into the rope belt she wore around her waist. She worked barefoot. When she was eleven or twelve, Minty began wearing a brightly colored bandanna around her head. This was a sign that she was no longer a child. Although she was barely five feet tall, Minty was a young woman now.

With the other field slaves, she sang as she worked. Her fine voice was distinctively husky as a result of her childhood bronchitis.

Most of the songs the slaves knew by heart were hymns. A favorite one told a popular Bible story:

> Oh, go down, Moses,
> Way down in Egypt land.
> Tell old Pharaoh,
> Let my people go. . . .

The white overseers, who watched the slaves to make sure they worked hard, were suspicious of this song. They feared that the slaves were really singing about themselves and how they wanted to be free.

Around this time several rumors found

their way to the Brodas plantation. One told about good people, both black and white, living in the North. They lived in states that were north of an imaginary boundary called the Mason-Dixon Line. In northern states, such as Pennsylvania, New York, and New Jersey, there were laws against slavery. Many people there hated the idea of slaves. They wanted to help slaves escape. Minty heard that these people had a special train. A slave could board it in the South and travel through a long, long tunnel to the North. When the slaves got off the train, they were free!

In fact, there was no such train. Yet in the early 1830s there was an organization of people who helped slaves escape. Some of them were free blacks. Some were former slaves who were now free. Some were Quakers and Methodists, whose religions told them that slavery was evil. Slave owners hated these people. They would do anything to stop them. So they had to operate in secret.

Sleek steam trains were new and exciting at this time. Everyone was talking about the railroad! A little more talk about trains wouldn't sound suspicious. So people invented a code name for helping slaves escape. They called it the "Underground Railroad."

Men and women called "conductors" drew maps to show slaves the safest ways to reach the North on foot. Or they drove them, hidden in carriages or wagons. "Train stations" were houses, barns, or churches where escaping slaves could hide and sleep during the day. The people who helped at the stations were called "stationmasters." The runaway slaves were called "passengers" or "parcels" or "freight." Big parcels were adult slaves; small ones were children. By speaking and writing letters using these code words, the people who ran the Underground Railroad kept it a secret.

The Underground Railroad was a slow way of freeing slaves. It was too slow for some people. They wanted slavery to be abolished immediately. Nat Turner, a slave in Virginia, was one of these people. He was a quiet, thoughtful man. He preached words from the Bible. One night he told six other slaves that he had had a vision from God. He believed that he was the man who would end slavery. To do this he said that God had told him to kill all the white people he could.

Nat Turner and a group of slaves set out by night to end slavery. They walked from one plantation to the next, killing white people and freeing their slaves. In all, they killed about sixty people. Then federal troops were called in to stop them. For a while Nat Turner hid out in a cave, but at last he was found and executed.

Word of Nat Turner's deeds spread like wildfire. Plantation owners feared other slaves might try to finish what Nat Turner had started. Nat Turner had been a preacher. He had spoken of the Children of Israel escaping slavery in the land of Egypt. This was dangerous! So slave owners passed a law forbidding slaves to go to church. They passed other laws saying that slaves could not get together to talk at all! It became a crime for anyone to teach a slave to read or write. And there was to be no more singing

> Oh, go down, Moses,
> Way down in Egypt land . . .

Yet the slaves found ways to gather and whisper together. Minty listened to their talk. It was frightening. But it was exciting, too. From that time on, she began to dream of freedom.

One day in the fall that Minty was thirteen, she was husking corn with slaves from some other plantations. She noticed a large black man who belonged to a farmer named Barrett. He wasn't singing with the other slaves. Minty seemed to have a sixth sense that told her when trouble was brewing. She kept her eye on the silent slave.

Suddenly Barrett's slave began to run. The overseer didn't see him until he was across a field. Then the overseer spurred his horse and took off, galloping after the slave.

Minty dropped the corn she was shucking. She ran after the overseer. She knew there was going to be terrible trouble. And she wanted to be there when it happened.

Barrett's slave came to a crossroads where there was a small village store. He ran inside to hide.

The overseer jumped off his horse and ran into the store after the slave. He waved his whip. He dragged Barrett's slave out from under the counter, where he was hiding, and yelled that he would whip him good.

Minty stepped into the store. The overseer

spotted her and called to her to help him tie up this slave so he could teach him a lesson. He expected Minty to obey him, so he eased his grip on the slave to ready his whip.

But Minty just stood there. She didn't move a muscle. Barrett's slave understood. She was giving him a chance to get away! Quickly he twisted away from the overseer and bolted out the door. He was off and running again!

The overseer started after him. But Minty stepped in front of him, blocking the doorway. When he saw that Minty wasn't going to let him through the door, the overseer grabbed a two-pound weight from the store's scale. He drew back his arm and heaved the weight at the runaway slave.

But the weight did not reach its target. Instead, it slammed into Minty's forehead! It knocked her to the ground, smashing her skull. Unconscious and bleeding, she was carried back to her cabin.

A few at a time Mr. Brodas's slaves stopped by Rit and Ben's cabin. They came to say goodbye to Minty. Surely she would die. Who could live with a hole in the middle of her forehead?

Once again Rit nursed Minty. She wept over her child. How she wanted her to live! But

if she did, surely she would be sold South. Mr. Brodas would never keep a slave who had refused to help his overseer.

For months Minty lay on a bed of rags in a deep, unnatural sleep. But somehow Rit managed to give her medicine and feed her.

After Christmas Mr. Brodas began bringing white men to see Minty. He was trying to sell her! He wasn't asking a high price. But the men laughed at Brodas. They wouldn't pay a penny for a half-dead slave.

By March it was plain that Minty was going to live. There was a large scar on her forehead. She suffered pounding headaches. She also had sudden sleeping spells. One moment she would be awake and talking, and then, right in the middle of a sentence, she would fall into a deep sleep. She never knew when these spells would come. But she wasn't going to die.

While Minty recuperated, she thought about things. She'd helped Barrett's slave to go free. Now she wanted freedom for herself. As a first step, she decided not to act like a slave anymore. Maybe Mr. Brodas could force her to work. But he couldn't make her smile at him or act like she was happy.

By early spring word reached the slave

quarter that Mr. Brodas planned to sell Minty and three of her brothers South. They would be going with the next chain gang. Minty was terrified! What would happen when she had one of her sleeping spells? She would fall down. The slave driver would whip her to make her get up. But she would be asleep! No doubt she would be whipped, then left to die on the road.

Often she'd prayed to the Lord to make her master a kind man. These prayers had not been answered. Now she said a different prayer. "Lord, if you're never going to change that man's heart—kill him, Lord, and take him out of the way." Minty repeated this prayer over and over.

The next week Minty heard that Mr. Brodas was ill. And shortly after that he died. Now Minty was sick at heart. To the end of her life she regretted her prayers for her master's death. She believed that her prayers had been answered.

John Tubman

Mr. Brodas's will stated that none of his slaves was to be sold South. Rit and Ben were happy to learn this. But Minty still worried. The word of a white man on paper didn't count for much when it came to black people. No one really knew what the new master, a minister called Dr. Anthony Thompson, might do.

The wound on Minty's head had healed. But strange dreams still troubled her. They seemed so real, like visions. She told the other slaves about her dreams. They listened. All the slaves admired this brave girl who had stood up to an overseer. The nickname "Minty" seemed too childish for this woman of courage. People began to call her Harriet.

When she was fit to work again, Harriet and her father, Ben, were hired out by Dr. Thompson to John Stewart, a builder. At first

Harriet was put to work cleaning his house. But after a few months she asked Mr. Stewart if she could work in the fields. He agreed. Stewart knew Harriet was strong. He'd seen her carry huge logs to the fireplace. And he wasn't paying much for Harriet. If she could work like a man, cutting trees and splitting timber, it would save him the money of hiring a more expensive male slave.

Harriet proved her worth as a strong field worker. In fact, she worked so well that Stewart allowed her to "hire her time." This meant that Harriet could take some extra jobs from other people on her own. She had to give Stewart part of the money she earned. But she was allowed to keep some for herself, too.

For six years Harriet labored for John Stewart. She never suspected that the hardship she endured and the discipline she learned were preparing her for the future.

Harriet was proud to be working with her father. Ben was in charge of the slaves who cut down trees for Mr. Stewart. He was a trusted slave, well known for his absolute honesty as well as his hard work.

But Ben could see that Harriet did not act like a slave. He knew that in her heart she longed for freedom. So, without ever saying a word, Ben began to teach her things as they worked in the woods. He taught her to imitate bird calls. He taught her which berries were safe to eat and which were poisonous. He taught her to travel through the woods without making any noise at all.

At night he showed her how to find the North Star. It always pointed to the North. Night travelers could keep the North Star in sight and be sure they were heading north. He showed her how to run her hand along a tree trunk, feeling for moss. Moss grew only on the north side of trees. If a night was cloudy and no stars could be seen, the moss could guide a traveler north as well as a star. In Harriet, Ben had a willing pupil.

Harriet found some satisfaction in plowing fields and cutting timber for Mr. Stewart. But she resented it terribly when he brought his white guests out to the fields to show off her strength. He ordered his overseer to harness Harriet like an ox to a heavy, stone-filled boat. Then the guests would gasp with astonishment as Harriet walked along the edge of the river, dragging the boat behind her. Mr. Stewart's little shows made Harriet feel no better than a beast. But there was nothing she could do about it.

In 1844, when Harriet was about twenty-three years old, she met a man named John Tubman. He was tall and handsome. He was always whistling cheerful tunes. John was black, but he wasn't a slave. He had been born free. His mother and father had belonged to a master who had died. The master's will had freed all his slaves. Although John was free and Harriet was a slave, he asked her to marry him.

Harriet accepted. She loved John deeply. She began to work very hard making a fine patchwork quilt for their marriage bed. It was the only beautiful thing Harriet ever owned. When they were married, Harriet Tubman took her quilt and went to live in John's cabin.

John never worried about anything. He seemed happy with their lives just the way they were. And he liked the extra money that Harriet was able to bring home from hiring out her time.

But Harriet worried. Her husband was free, yet she was still a slave. The plantation

STEVEN JAMES PETRUCCIO

wasn't making enough money. Soon, Harriet knew, Dr. Thompson would start selling his slaves. What if he decided to sell her?

Harriet told John her worries. She told him her nightmares of slave traders coming with whips and chains. She wanted him to run away with her, to follow the North Star to freedom. But John shrugged her worries away. He was happy where he was. They had a little money, didn't they? And a cabin of their own?

Not all Harriet's dreams were bad. Some were dreams of freedom, visions of flying free over the cotton fields and mountains. As she flew in her dreams, she came to a wall that she couldn't fly over. Just as she was about to fall, she saw women all dressed in white on the other side of the wall. They held out their arms to her. They wanted to pull her over the wall to freedom.

When Harriet told John about her flying dreams, he said they were crazy. At last he grew tired of hearing them. He said that if she tried to run away, he would tell the master.

Harriet was shocked. Would her own hus-band betray her? He must have been joking. She looked up into the eyes of this tall man whom she loved so much. There she saw only a cold glare. Harriet was more hurt by John's words than she'd ever been by Miss Susan's whip. From that moment on Harriet was afraid of John Tubman.

Go Free or Die!

Freedom. The word was always on Harriet's mind now. She'd often heard her mother complain that she was supposed to be free. Now Harriet decided to find out if this was true. With the money she made hiring out her time, she paid a lawyer five dollars, a large sum in those days. He looked in the record books. He discovered that Rit's first owner had died. In his will he left Rit to a woman named Mary Patterson. Rit was to serve Mary until she was forty-five. But Mary died young. Since there was no word about Rit in her will, Rit legally became free when she died.

Rit should have been free! But no one had told her. She had been tricked! Another owner had snatched her up, and she remained a slave. Harriet realized that papers and contracts were white men's tools. She couldn't trust them to make her free. She would have to try another way.

Early one morning Harriet was working in a field that was close to a road. A neighboring white woman drove up in a buggy. She wore the plain dress of a Quaker. Seeing that no one was around, the woman stopped and spoke to Harriet. She asked her name and how she had gotten the scar on her head. Harriet told the woman her story. She knew that Quakers didn't believe in slavery and could be trusted. After this the woman made a habit of talking to Harriet when no one was watching. Once she whispered that if Harriet ever needed help, she could come to her farm near Bucktown. Bucktown, Maryland, was a tiny town near Dr. Thompson's plantation.

Harriet was grateful to the white woman. Yet she knew that escape would be especially dangerous for her. She might have one of her spells and be caught while sleeping on the road. With the big scar on her forehead, she would be easy to recognize. So, for the time being, Harriet kept the Quaker woman's words a secret in her heart.

News soon came to the plantation that a slave trader from the South had arrived. Some-

one whispered to Harriet that she and three of her brothers were to be sold to him. Sold South! Harriet ran to find her brothers. She told them what she had learned. They must run away!

That night Harriet waited until her husband, John, fell asleep. Then she slid silently out of their cabin. She met her brothers, and they started off through the woods. Harriet took the lead. She knew the woods. They did not. Every owl that hooted, every frog that croaked startled them. They did not move very fast. And to Harriet they seemed to stomp and crash like a herd of cattle!

Harriet kept encouraging them on. But at last her brothers stopped. They were frightened. They were going back.

Harriet began to protest. They must go on!

But her brothers were firm. It was too risky.

At last Harriet said that she was going North alone. But her brothers didn't think she should. They grabbed her. She fought them tooth and nail, but three men were too many for her. They forced her to walk back to the plantation.

Only two days passed before a little water boy whispered more news to Harriet as she worked in the field. She and her brothers had been sold. The slave trader was coming for them that same night!

What was she to do? If she stayed, she would be put in the chain gang. She knew she would die on the long walk South. But if she ran, who would go with her? Not her three brothers. Not her husband. John might even help the men with guns and bloodhounds who were sure to come after her! If Harriet ran, she would be all alone.

"There's one of two things I've got a *right* to, liberty or death," Harriet explained years later. "If I could not have one, I would have the other. No man will take me back alive."

Harriet straightened up and walked away from the field. She must let someone know that she was leaving. Otherwise, her family might think she was headed South with the dreaded chain gang.

Harriet saw Rit walking toward her on her way to milk a cow. But she knew she couldn't tell her mother. Rit would make a great fuss.

As Rit drew near, Harriet told her to go back to the cabin. Harriet said that she would do the milking that night. This was Harriet's good-bye to her mother.

After she milked the cow, Harriet went to

the Big House. She planned to find her sister Mary, who worked there. She could trust Mary with her secret.

Mary was in the kitchen, but several other slaves were, too. Harriet needed to tell Mary in private, so she pretended to wrestle with her sister. She pulled her outside, away from the others.

Harriet was about to tell Mary that she was running away. But before she could, Dr. Thompson rode up to the house on his horse. He would not be happy to see two slaves chatting during working hours. Mary made a dash for the kitchen. As she hurried away, Harriet did the only thing she could think of. She began to sing:

> I'm sorry, friends, to leave you,
> Farewell! Oh, farewell!
> But I'll meet you in the morning,
> Farewell! Oh, farewell!
>
> I'll meet you in the morning,
> When you reach the Promised Land;
> On the other side of Jordan,
> For I'm bound for the Promised Land!

That evening Harriet did nothing to call attention to herself. She went to bed as usual and waited until she was sure John was sleeping soundly. Then she got up. She packed a little corn bread and salt pork in a bandanna. Then she folded up the beautiful quilt she had made. She was taking it with her.

Silently Harriet made her way through the dark woods. She remembered how Ben had told her that even bloodhounds couldn't follow a scent through water, so Harriet waded in streams whenever possible. Her long skirt heavy with mud, she came to the farmhouse of the Quaker woman. Trembling, she knocked on the door.

When the Quaker woman saw that it was Harriet, she quickly let her in. But the woman told Harriet that it wasn't safe for her to stay at the farmhouse. Harriet must travel on that very night.

The Quaker woman explained to Harriet that she had more than ninety miles to go before she would cross the Mason-Dixon Line to freedom. First, she must follow the Choptank River north for forty miles. The river would become narrower as it reached its source. When the river ended, Harriet should follow the road to Camden, Delaware. Just outside of the town she should look for a white house with green shutters. On a small slip of paper the woman wrote down a message for the Hunns, the people who lived in the white house. When she got there, Harriet should give the paper to them. They would tell her what to do next. The Hunns' house would be Harriet's first stop on the Underground Railroad.

As Harriet was leaving the farmhouse, she felt very grateful to the Quaker woman for helping her. She wanted to repay her kindness. She had no money, but she had one thing she valued. Harriet gave the woman her beautiful quilt.

Crossing the Line

Harriet started off again through the woods. All night she walked north, wading in the Choptank whenever possible. As the sun began to rise, Harriet dug a hole in the underbrush. She climbed in and pulled some grass and weeds over her head. There, she rested as best she could through the day.

In the evening Harriet began following the river again. By now she knew she must be missed. Dr. Thompson would have slave hunters and dogs out looking for her. She quickened her step, alert for any unfamiliar sound in the woods.

At times Harriet's path north led her to a road. Then she would watch and listen for some time. Not until she was sure the coast was clear would she race across.

Finally the river narrowed, just as the Quaker woman had said it would. At last it was just a trickle, and beyond it Harriet saw a dirt road. Taking a last drink from the Choptank and pulling her bandanna down to hide her scar, Harriet walked swiftly along the side of the dark road. And then, without warning, a sleeping spell came on. Harriet sank to the ground, unconscious.

When she woke up, it was still pitch dark. But she heard men's voices and horses snuffling and stomping on the road. She dared not move a muscle. The men were slave hunters! She could hear them talking about a runaway girl!

Then one of the men told the others that they should turn back. They would start hunting again early in the morning. And they would bring their dogs with them, too.

Harriet's heart pounded as she listened to the men ride off. When she was sure that they were far away, she got up and began running toward Camden again. Now she must find the Hunns' house before morning!

But the sun rose before Harriet reached the white house with green shutters. She saw a woman in the yard feeding chickens. Harriet began to panic. What if this wasn't the right white house? What if this woman wasn't Mrs. Hunn? Fearfully Harriet approached the house.

The woman looked up and saw the tired, dusty runaway walking toward her.

Without speaking, Harriet held out the slip of paper to her. The woman read it and then smiled.

"Welcome, Harriet," she said. "I am Eliza Hunn. I am glad to see thee."

Harriet knew from the way Eliza Hunn said *thee* instead of *you* that she was a Quaker. She led Harriet inside her house and fixed her breakfast.

Harriet stayed for three days with Eliza Hunn and her husband, Ezekiel. She ate her meals with them, and they talked. Most of the time Harriet stayed hidden inside the house. But when she wanted some fresh air, she took a broom and swept the Hunn's yard. No one passing the house would think that the black girl sweeping the yard could be a runaway slave. And for the first time Harriet slept in a real bed at night.

The fourth night Eliza gave Harriet freshly washed clothes and packed up a parcel of food.

Then Ezekiel helped her climb into the back of his wagon. He covered her with a blanket.

Ezekiel drove the wagon through the little town of Camden. On the far side he stopped the wagon beside some woods. Making sure no one was on the road, he told Harriet to climb out. He explained that it wasn't safe for him to drive her any farther. Slave hunters were everywhere in these parts. The best thing for her to do was walk north through the woods to Wilmington, Delaware. Just before Wilmington she would see a cemetery. That was where she should wait for the next conductor. Ezekiel told her it would take two nights of walking.

After thanking Ezekiel, Harriet turned and disappeared into the woods. Once again she walked all night, following the North Star. She thanked God for bringing her this far. At dawn Harriet hid in a hollow tree and waited for sundown.

After another long night's walk Harriet reached a graveyard. There she saw a man. He was muttering to himself. Harriet wondered if he was crazy. But as she drew closer, she made out the words he was saying over and over. "I

have a ticket for the railroad. I have a ticket for the railroad." Joyfully Harriet walked up to him.

The man introduced himself to Harriet as Mr. Trent. He handed her men's work clothes and explained that she was to disguise herself as his workman. Quickly Harriet put on the clothes, laced up a pair of work boots, and pulled a man's hat down to hide her scar. With a shovel over her shoulder, Harriet followed Mr. Trent into Wilmington.

In the busy city no one looked twice at the black man with the shovel. Mr. Trent led Harriet to a house next to a small shoe shop and knocked.

"I have a shipment for you," Mr. Trent told the man who opened the door. "One bale of cotton."

The man nodded. Thanking Mr. Trent, Harriet slipped inside the house.

Harriet stayed in Thomas Garrett's house all day. He was another Quaker, well known for helping slaves. Because he owned a shoe factory, he always supplied runaways with a new pair of much-needed shoes for their journey.

The next evening, a Sunday night, Mr. Garrett gave Harriet fancy women's clothes to wear. He gave her gloves and a hat with a thick veil. When she was dressed, Harriet sat right up beside Mr. Garrett as he drove his buggy through town. In her elegant clothes, no one would guess that Mr. Garrett's companion was a runaway.

Just north of Wilmington Mr. Garrett stopped the buggy. He gave Harriet a piece of paper with the word *Pennsylvania* printed on it. He knew that Harriet couldn't read. But he whispered to her that she would come to a sign-post farther down the road. He told her to check the sign for the word that was printed on the piece of paper. When she crossed that road, she would be in a free state. Then she should walk the short distance from the sign to the city of Philadelphia.

Mr. Garrett told her that this was the most dangerous part of the journey, even though it wasn't far to Pennsylvania. Slave hunters watched the Pennsylvania border like hawks.

In the dark Harriet started up the road. She was close to freedom! But all of a sudden her sixth sense sent her a warning. Harriet dashed into the woods and hid. A few minutes later she heard horses galloping along the road. She stayed hidden until all was quiet. Then she ran through the woods, not stopping until she came to the road.

The sun was just coming up as she held the slip of paper up to the signpost. The words were the same! In another minute Harriet crossed the magical Mason-Dixon Line!

Later Harriet told how it felt. "I looked at my hands to see if I was the same person now that I was free. There was such a glory over everything, the sun came like gold through the trees, and over the fields, and I felt like I was in Heaven."

Harriet was no longer a slave. She was free! Yet the wonder faded when Harriet realized just where her long, dangerous journey had brought her. Years afterward she said, "I had crossed the line of which I had so long been dreaming. I was free, but there was no one to welcome me to the land of freedom. I was a stranger in a strange land, and my home, after all, was down in the old cabin quarter, and the old folks and my brothers and my sisters and friends were there. But I was free. And they should be free also!" Harriet made a vow at that moment. Someday she would return to Maryland. She would gather her family around her. And she would lead them to freedom.

Another Escape

Harriet didn't need to hide as she walked to Philadelphia. There was no reason to fear slave catchers or their baying dogs. She was a free woman in a free state!

In Philadelphia Harriet took a job in a hotel. For the first time in her life Harriet kept all the money she earned. She cooked, dusted, swept, and scrubbed. She worked inside, though she didn't enjoy it. But she knew she'd need money to return to slave territory. So she kept working, thinking about the day when she would rescue her family. When she found a job that wasn't to her liking, Harriet simply quit and found another. She enjoyed this part of her new freedom.

The city of Philadelphia was a center for abolitionists, people who believed that slavery should not exist. It was also a center for runaway slaves. Harriet marveled at the many well-dressed, well-spoken black people she saw there.

An important organization in Philadelphia in 1850 was the Vigilance Committee. This was a group of people who helped runaway slaves. It was headed by a black man, William Still. Harriet often went to the offices of the Vigilance Committee. She got to know William Still. He found people to write letters that Harriet dictated. He had ways of getting them to her family back in Maryland. He also helped Harriet get news from her family.

Once when Harriet went to visit William Still, he told her that trouble was brewing for her family. Her sister Mary was married to John Bowley, a free Negro. They had two children. John heard that his family was going to be sold South, so he went to a Quaker and asked for help. The Quaker was an agent for the Underground Railroad. He sent a message to William Still. But he couldn't write what John Bowley had told him. Someone might read his mail. Then they would know that John Bowley was trying to help his family escape! Instead, the Quaker wrote that there were two large bales of wool and two small bales of wool that needed to be sent from Baltimore to Philadelphia.

When Harriet heard this, she declared that she was going back to Maryland. She was going to lead her sister, her brother-in-law, and their children to freedom. William Still tried to talk Harriet out of this plan. After all, she was wanted in Maryland. Once she crossed south of the Mason-Dixon Line, the slave hunters might catch her.

But Harriet was firm. She was going to be the one to get those bales of wool to Pennsylvania.

Coded letters went back and forth from Maryland to Philadelphia. Harriet and her Quaker friend at last had a plan to help Mary and the children escape. They sent John Bowley the plan. But by that time his wife and children were about to be sold. They had been taken to the slave pens at the courthouse in Cambridge. The slave auction had already started! But luckily, it began with the sale of the strong field hands who were worth the most money. The less valuable property, women and children, had to wait in the pen all morning.

At lunchtime the auctioneer went off to a

nearby inn to eat. He would finish the auction after lunch.

John Bowley watched the auctioneer leave the courthouse. Then, holding a large white envelope that his Quaker friend had given him, he walked boldly to the slave pens. Trying to look official, he handed the envelope to the guard at the pens. He said that his master wanted him to bring a woman and her two children over to the inn because he thought he had a buyer for them.

The guard read the message that John's Quaker friend had written. Then he nodded and gave the envelope back to John. He opened the gate and John went in. He shoved his wife and gruffly told her and the children to get along.

If Mary was surprised by her husband's rude behavior, she didn't let on. She merely followed John, carrying the baby. Their older child clung to her skirt. Forcing himself not to run, John led his family calmly down the main street of town. If anyone came out to question them, they might be caught! Here they were, escaping in broad daylight!

After what seemed like a long walk, they reached a house with a picket fence. John pushed open the gate and hurried his family inside. There his Quaker friend was waiting. He took them up to his attic, where they hid until dark.

After a quick supper the Quaker put the family in the back of a wagon, hidden under many blankets. Then he drove them to the river. He rowed them in a dinghy to the middle of the river, where a fishing boat was waiting, stocked with food and blankets. John was to sail the boat up the Chesapeake River. When he got near Baltimore, he would see two lights, one blue and one yellow. Then he was to get into the little rowboat attached to the fishing boat and row ashore.

John sailed all night. As the day began to dawn, he worried that he wouldn't be able to see the lights. But at last he spotted them and rowed his family toward the lights.

As the family approached the shore, they saw a large white woman sitting in a wagon.

"Who are you?" she asked.

John did not know what to think. Would this woman understand the password he had been told to say? "A friend with friends," John said softly.

"God bless you, you made it!" said the white

53

woman. "I've been waiting for two mornings straight."

Once again John and his family found themselves in the back of a wagon. This time they were covered with onions and potatoes as well as blankets. The big woman drove them to a stable and hustled them inside. She gave them a bundle of food, and they waited there all day.

At nightfall they climbed into the wagon once more. This time they drove to a brick house. The white woman knocked on the door, and then they all went in.

Suddenly Mary cried out, "Harriet!"

Harriet was the one who had made the arrangements for the boats and the wagon. Now she was there to lead them to freedom on the Underground Railroad.

Harriet had used some of the money she'd earned to buy a pistol. Armed with this and her knowledge of the swampland, Harriet led Mary and her family from station to station. Hiding by day and traveling by night, the party made their way north. Sometimes they traveled on foot, and other times they rode in wagons or boats. At last they arrived safely in Pennsylvania. This was Harriet's first trip as a conductor of the Underground Railroad.

All Aboard!

Just as Harriet began her career as a conductor, leading slaves to freedom, the Fugitive Slave Law was passed. Now it was the duty of all citizens, even those living north of the Mason-Dixon Line, to help capture runaways. If people refused to obey the new law, they would have to pay big fines or go to jail.

Captured blacks were brought before a special commissioner. It was his job to decide if they were runaway slaves or free blacks. The commissioner was paid for his work. He got five dollars for declaring that a captive was a freeman. He got ten dollars for saying that a captive was a runaway slave! Of course, most captives were declared runaways and sent back to the South.

Another part of the law said that anyone sheltering a runaway slave would be thrown into prison. It became very dangerous to be part of the Underground Railroad. Now, even in Philadelphia, Harriet could be arrested at any time.

But this new law did not stop Harriet. She still planned to return to slave territory, even though it was far more hazardous for her now. She was determined to bring the rest of her family to freedom. Only now they would have to travel almost twice as far to be free. They would have to go all the way to Canada.

In the spring of 1851 Harriet traveled back to Maryland. She led one of her brothers and two other men safely North.

That summer Harriet worked in another hotel. She saved every penny she earned. She was going South a third time, and this time she planned to bring out John Tubman.

It was two years since she'd seen her husband. In that time her fear of him had faded. She remembered only his handsome face, his easy laugh, his merry whistling. She was sure she could persuade him to go North with her. They would live in freedom together. They would have a family.

With these thoughts in her head, Harriet returned to the plantation where she had grown up. Dr. Thompson would never expect to see her back there again! But to make sure she wasn't recognized, she wore a man's suit. A man's felt hat hid the scar on her forehead.

Late at night Harriet knocked on the door of their old cabin. John answered the door, but only stared at her. Who was this short man standing before him?

"It's me," she whispered. "Harriet!" She held out her hands to him.

But John didn't take her hands. Instead, he put his arm around a young woman who had come to stand beside him at the door.

"I came back for you, John," Harriet said.

John shook his head. "This is Caroline," he said, nodding toward the young woman. "Caroline is my wife now. I'm not going North or anywhere else. I wouldn't leave here for anything in the world."

Then John laughed, and Caroline joined him.

Harriet just stood there, at the door. She was dressed in rumpled, dirty men's clothing. She felt old and ugly compared to Caroline. Her dream of a life with the man she loved was crushed.

Harriet turned away from John's cabin. He

had hurt her before. But this time was so much worse!

Harriet hurried off into the cover of darkness. Maybe John would tell Dr. Thompson that she was there. She didn't plan to stay around and find out.

A few hours later Harriet had managed to gather a group of slaves together. These slaves wanted freedom, so Harriet led them North.

For the next seven years Harriet's life took on a pattern. She spent the winters in St. Catharines, Canada. It was a good place for black people. They could earn money and buy homes. Harriet rented a house there, and several former slaves moved in with her. In the cold Canadian winter they chopped wood to earn money. In the spring and summer Harriet worked in Cape May, New Jersey, or in Philadelphia, Pennsylvania, cooking and cleaning in hotels. She was taking a big risk, and she had to be careful to hide her telltale scar. But Harriet was used to danger. She needed the money she earned to pay for her trips back to slave country. During this time she made two trips each year.

In 1854 word reached Harriet in Canada

that three of her brothers—Benjamin, William Henry, and John—had been sold South. They were to be put on the chain gang the day after Christmas. This did not give Harriet much time. But she arranged for the brothers to meet her on Christmas morning at her parents' house. Ben and Rit now lived near a timber area forty miles north of Dr. Thompson's plantation.

Early on December twenty-fifth Harriet slipped into a shed outside her parents' cabin to find shelter from the rain. With her were her brothers, two other men, and a woman, the fiancée of one of her brothers. Harriet peeked out through gaps in the shed walls. She saw Ben doing chores. He had aged in the five years since she'd seen him. Harriet saw Rit bustling around the cabin. Rit had killed a pig for Christmas dinner. She was expecting her three sons to arrive at any minute.

How Harriet longed to run to her parents and throw her arms around them! But she knew she couldn't. If her mother found out she was there, she would shout with joy. Other slaves in nearby cabins might hear her, and it would endanger their escape.

So Harriet sent the two men her parents

didn't know to the cabin. They asked to speak to Ben outside so Rit wouldn't hear. They told him who was in his shed and what they were trying to do.

Ben went back to his cabin. Without Rit seeing, he gathered up some of the Christmas dinner. Then he took it to the shed door. He slipped the food inside. But he did not go in himself.

Ben knew that Dr. Thompson would soon notice that three of his sons were missing. Right away he would ride out to Ben's cabin. And he would ask Ben if he had seen his sons. Ben didn't want to lie. He was known for his honesty. He knew he had to be able to say truthfully that he had not seen his children.

Ben made several trips out to the shed that Christmas. He brought whatever he thought would help his children. Poor old Rit rocked back and forth in front of the fireplace all day worrying about where her boys could be.

It was still raining hard at dusk. It was time for the runaways to be on their way. Ben walked with them a little way, wearing a blindfold. Harriet held one of his arms as they walked. She told him about her trips North. And she said that sometime soon she would come back for him and Rit.

After a while Ben stopped and the others went on without him. He waited until he could no longer hear their footsteps. Then he took off his blindfold and walked home.

The next day some slave hunters came with Dr. Thompson to Ben's cabin. They questioned Ben and Rit.

Rit shook her head. "Not one of my children came this Christmas," she complained. "I was looking out for them all day, and my heart's almost broke about them not coming."

Dr. Thompson turned to Ben. "Have you seen them?" he asked.

"No," said Ben. "I haven't seen them."

Ben's word was good enough for Dr. Thompson. The slave hunters did not search the woods north of Ben's cabin. In this way Ben helped his children escape. And even though she didn't know it, Rit's heartbreaking but truthful answer helped, too.

"General Moses" Tubman

Harriet's trips South were like military campaigns, raids into armed enemy territory. No two trips were alike. Each time Harriet brought slaves North, she traveled a different route. She got to know every swamp, riverbank, Quaker meetinghouse, and potato hole along the Eastern Seaboard.

Harriet had many ways to help her "passengers" slip by slave hunters. Sometimes she dressed men in women's clothes. Other times women wore men's clothes. Often she led slaves away on a Saturday night. Sundays were not work days. The slaves probably wouldn't be missed. And slave owners wouldn't be able to organize a search party or have Wanted posters printed up describing the runaways until Monday. By that time the slaves would be far away.

Harriet led many men and women out of

slavery. She also carried many "small parcels." But she couldn't take a chance of a baby crying while the runaways were in hiding. The whole party might be caught. So Harriet made sure that when babies were along, she had plenty of paregoric with her. This all-purpose medicine had some opium in it. It made the babies fall into a deep sleep. Then Harriet would slip them into a bag she carried around her waist. She could trek through fields and wade rivers with her slumbering parcels safe and sound—and quiet.

Occasionally Harriet arranged for slaves to begin their journey North by hitching up their master's horse and buggy. She had them drive right through town in broad daylight. Harriet knew that the slaves would look as if they were running an errand for their master. No one would suspect that they would be bold enough to run away like this!

Harriet knew people who could forge train passes. Some of the passes said that the run-aways were free Negroes. Others said that they were slaves, traveling North with their master's permission. Sometimes Harriet went with her runaways on real, above-ground railroads. But this was very risky. Posters with drawings of

Harriet were often tacked up at train stations. Sometimes when Harriet could sense that danger was ahead, she would take her runaways off a train at the next stop. She would have them board a southbound train. Who would ever be looking for runaway slaves headed *south*?

Harriet could quickly size up a group of runaways. Some of them showed great courage and determination to be free. As she led them, she would show them the things that Ben had shown her so long ago: how to navigate by the North Star, how moss grows only on the north side of a tree, how to signal one another using the call of a hoot owl or a whippoorwill. When she thought they were ready to travel on their own, she would give them directions and names of people who would help them. As they headed North, Harriet would turn back to slave country again, to collect more passengers for the Underground Railroad.

Other groups of slaves needed Harriet to lead them the whole way. It was easy to become discouraged by the hardships they endured. Often winds raged and snow blinded them for days at a time, and runaways had little to keep them warm. They could not build a fire, because a slave hunter might see it. It was hard to sleep in the daytime, when every little rustle of leaves might be a bloodhound on their trail. Runaways frequently became exhausted and were often on the brink of starvation. When their spirits failed, Harriet had to keep them going. At these times she would tell them wonderful stories about how it felt to be free. In Canada they could work at any job they wished. If they didn't like it, they could change to another. In Canada black people earned money and bought their own houses. They sent their children to school to learn to read and write.

But sometimes even Harriet's stories were not enough to keep a runaway going. On one trip she and eleven slaves had to hide in a swamp for a whole day. They were wet and uncomfortable. They had nothing to eat. When night came, Harriet whispered that it was time to go. But one man refused. He'd had enough of this starving and hiding in swamps! He wasn't going with them and that was final.

A slave who went back was dangerous. His master would beat him until he told what route the runaways had taken, where their hiding places were, and the names of those who had helped them. Harriet wasn't about to let this one frightened man endanger the lives of so many others. As he stood where he was, Harriet stepped up to him. She put her pistol to his head. "Move or die!" she said, pointing north. He moved. A few days later he was a free man in Canada.

On these treacherous trips Harriet would often be seized by sleeping spells. They could last a few minutes or several hours. While she slept, her followers waited patiently. No one tried to take away her pistol or go on without her. They trusted her to lead them safely to freedom.

Word of Harriet's trips spread throughout the South. Slaves talked of her courage. They began to call her Moses because she was leading her people to freedom. Legends began to grow about her. Some said that she could see in the dark like a mule. Others said she could catch the scent of danger on the wind like a fox. Still others said that she was strong enough to pick up a man and carry him over her shoulder for miles.

When Harriet was told these stories of her great daring, she would shake her head. "It wasn't me," she protested. "It was the Lord." People who knew her well realized that Harriet put her trust firmly in God. She simply expected miracles to happen!

Slaves weren't the only ones to hear about Harriet. Slave owners heard of Moses, too. They wondered who this powerful man could be who stole their valuable property away. For a long time they didn't know that Moses was Harriet. But at last they learned the truth. Then they put up posters offering big rewards for the capture of Harriet "Moses" Tubman. At one point Harriet was worth a total of forty thousand dollars in rewards! She was wanted dead or alive. Most of the slave owners hoped it would be dead. But it didn't really matter. If she was caught still breathing, she would be hanged. Or better yet, burned alive at the stake.

Slavers tacked Wanted posters of Harriet to trees along major roads. A drawing of a stocky black woman with a scar on her forehead wearing a bandanna appeared on the posters. Below the drawing a caption told that Harriet was about thirty-five years old. Her height was five feet. And it said that she could neither read nor write.

Harriet heard about these posters. Now that people krew Moses was a middle-aged woman, she often dressed as a man or disguised

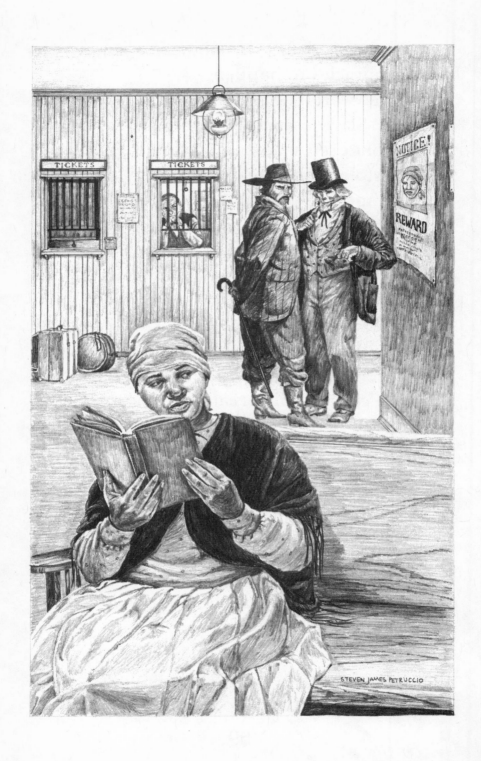

STEVEN JAMES PETRUCCIO

herself as an old woman. She would often pay some small black boy to follow after the poster hangers. As soon as they were out of sight, he would rip the posters down.

One time Harriet was sitting at a train station when she overheard two men talking about her. They were trying to decide if she was the woman on the poster. Harriet had a book under her arm. Slowly she took it out and opened it.

"No," she heard one of the men say at last. "She's reading. And that poster said the one they're after can't read."

Harriet breathed a sigh of relief. The whole time the men were talking, she had been praying that she was holding the book right side up!

The Final Trips

During the late 1850s Harriet continued sneaking back to "the land of Egypt," as she called Maryland, and leading slaves to "the promised land" of freedom. She'd taken field hands, cooks, and housemaids. She'd taken their young children and their tiny babies. But now she had a new kind of passenger for her train. These passengers wouldn't be able to wade across rivers or walk through swamps all night. They couldn't run quickly if there was danger.

These passengers were Harriet's elderly parents, Ben and Rit. Harriet had some disturbing dreams about them. Then she found out that Ben was in trouble. She had to take them North. But to do it, Harriet had to come up with some new ways to travel. Trusting in the Lord to help her as always, Harriet set out for Maryland.

When she reached Bucktown, it was daylight. She hoped that she wouldn't run into Dr. Thompson. But just in case, she invented a disguise. First, she bought two live chickens and tied them by their feet with a cord. She tied the cord to her belt. Next, she pulled her wide sunbonnet down to hide her face and stooped over when she walked. Now she looked just like a little old woman taking her chickens to market.

As she was rounding a corner, she saw Dr. Thompson on his horse heading right for her. Keeping her head down, she yanked the cord holding the chickens. Away they flapped. Harriet waved her hands in mock distress and ran off after them.

Dr. Thompson laughed as he watched the scene. "Go, Granny!" he called after her, never suspecting that this woman had once been his property.

Harriet hid in the nearby woods until dark. Then she made her way to Ben and Rit's cabin. Softly she knocked on the door.

Rit let her in. Harriet was worried that her

STEVEN JAMES PETRUCCIO

mother would be so overjoyed to see her that she'd cause an uproar. But Rit simply hugged her and told her about Ben's trouble.

Another of Mr. Barrett's slaves, a man named Peter, had tried to run away. He hid in Ben's corncrib. Ben never went to the corncrib except when it was pitch dark. So he never "saw" Peter. But he put some food into the corncrib for him.

After a few days Peter changed his mind about running away. He went back home. He told his wife where he had been. His wife thought maybe she could gain favor with Mr. Barrett, so she told him that old Ben had helped Peter.

Now Dr. Thompson and Mr. Barrett were calling Ben up to the Big House every day. They were questioning him. Rit was afraid that they might sell him South or put him in jail. Harriet had arrived in the nick of time.

When her father came home, Harriet again thought how her parents had aged even in the few years since she'd seen them. How was she ever going to get them all the way to Canada? She decided that she would need a horse.

Harriet told her parents to get ready for a trip. Then she walked over to the Barrett plantation. There she found an old horse named Dollie Mae. She coaxed the horse to her feet and rode her into the woods. Harriet tied Dollie Mae to a tree not far from Ben and Rit's cabin.

Harriet scouted around until she found an old pair of carriage wheels on an axle. She fastened a board over the axle and, with rope, hung a second board down below the first. Now the old people could sit on one board and rest their feet on the other.

After dark Harriet hitched Dollie Mae to her makeshift wagon. Then she ran to get her parents. Ben brought his axe. Rit carried the feather comforter she had made. With these few belongings, they climbed up onto the wagon seat. Harriet took the reins and off they rode into the night.

All night long they traveled north in the crude wagon. At daybreak Harriet pulled far into the woods and they slept. That night they headed north again. They traveled on for two more nights. Finally they arrived in Wilmington. There Harriet's old friend, Thomas Garrett, gave the two old people money and train passes. Ben and Rit rode in comfort the rest of the way to Canada.

Harriet couldn't go with them. It was too dangerous for her to travel out in the open now. By night she traveled to Canada on foot and in friends' wagons. She met her parents in the little town of St. Catharines. Ben and Rit were free!

Harriet settled her parents in her small rented house. They spent a hard, frigid winter there. Ben and Rit were not used to cold weather. When spring came, Harriet moved her parents down to a little house on South Street in Auburn, New York. It was risky to settle there, with the Fugitive Slave Law still in effect. But Harriet had many powerful friends in New York State. She knew they would help her if she was in trouble.

Harriet had always lived on very little money herself. She used her earnings for her trips to "Egypt land." But now she had her parents to support. She took several part-time jobs. She sometimes spoke at antislavery meetings and was able to earn extra money.

When Harriet traveled to one of these meetings, she carried letters of introduction. She also took along pictures of the friends who had arranged for her to speak. When she met new people, she would show them a picture. If they could name her friend in the picture, Harriet knew that she could trust them.

Shy at first, Harriet soon became a fine speaker. She had a wonderful memory and was a natural storyteller. She held her audiences spellbound with tales of her narrow escapes leading slaves to freedom.

By 1860 the United States was very close to war. People living in states in the North disagreed violently with those living in states in the South. Slavery was one of the main issues. Now the pro-slavers wanted all the freed blacks returned to their masters. More slave hunters than ever roamed the highways in the North. Every day runaways were caught and sent back into slavery.

Of course, Harriet didn't let the danger stop her from going where she wanted to go. That year she was traveling to Boston to speak. On the way she stopped to visit a relative in Troy, New York. There, Charles Nalle, an ex-slave, had been caught by a slave hunter. He was being held at the courthouse. His hearing was about to begin. A commissioner would decide if Nalle should be sent back South.

A group of abolitionists waited in the

square outside the courthouse. Pro-slavers waited, too. There were about a thousand people in all. Tempers were high.

Harriet had the feeling that something important was going to happen. She arranged for a boat to be waiting on the riverbank, just in case. Then she had some little boys run around the town shouting, "Fire! Fire!" Soon alarm bells began to ring. Just as Harriet hoped, more and more people poured into the square.

Harriet pulled down her sunbonnet once again. She bent over like a weak old woman. No one who saw her could have imagined how strong she really was! Acting like an old lady, Harriet elbowed her way through the crowd. She made her way past the guards until she was inside the courtroom itself.

Suddenly a voice from the crowd out in the square called, "We will buy Nalle's freedom! What is his master's price?"

The slave hunter walked to the courtroom window. "Twelve hundred dollars!" he called out to the crowd.

Someone in the crowd began collecting money. Wealthy people gave generously. Poor people gave what they could. Little by little, twelve hundred dollars was collected.

"We have raised twelve hundred dollars!" the voice announced. The crowd cheered.

The slave hunter went to the window again. It had not taken these people very long to come up with twelve hundred dollars. No doubt they could come up with more. "Fifteen hundred dollars!" he shouted.

What a greedy cheat! Going back on his word! The crowd was furious. They pressed forward.

Inside the courthouse the commissioner told the guards to lead Charles Nalle away. He was an escaped slave and must be sent back South. That was the law.

The guards began to take the handcuffed Nalle out the door. But the "old woman" suddenly sprang forward. She ran to the window. "Here he comes!" Harriet shouted to the crowd. "Take him!"

Then Harriet ran out of the courthouse. "General" Tubman began giving orders to the crowd. "This man shall not go back to slavery!" she shouted. "Take him, friends! Drag him to the river!"

Harriet pounced on one of the guards holding the prisoner. He hit her head with his wooden club. But Harriet never flinched. She took Nalle's arm and slipped her hand inside his handcuff. Attached to him, she pulled him through the mob.

A little farther on, a guard knocked Harriet and Nalle to the ground. Harriet quickly snatched off her bonnet. She put it on Nalle's head. When they stood up, no one could tell where Nalle was in the sea of people. Harriet pulled Charles Nalle through a crowd of people waving clubs and firing pistols. At last they reached the Hudson River.

Back in the courthouse the commissioner saw what was happening. He telegraphed the police station on the other side of the river. As the boat carrying Harriet and Nalle landed on the opposite shore, many policemen were there to meet them. They recaptured Nalle and put him in jail.

But many angry abolitionists had crossed the river, too. They marched to the jail and threw rocks at the door. The policemen fired their guns into the crowd.

"They can only kill a dozen of us!" someone shouted. "Come on!"

More shots rang out. Many people were killed. At last a very large black man pushed open the prison door. But the sheriff was waiting inside with a hatchet. He swung the hatchet, splitting open the big man's head. The man slumped to the ground, dead. His big body blocked the door. The sheriff couldn't close it. A wave of people rushed in. Harriet was among them. They grabbed Nalle a second time and carried him out of the jail.

On the street they hailed a man driving by. When he heard their story, the man jumped down and gave them his horse and buggy. The abolitionists drove Nalle out of town.

Nalle was safe. But Harriet was in more danger than ever. The police were looking for the "little old lady" who had started all the trouble. She could be arrested. So her friends hid her just outside of Troy. They nursed her battle wounds. Two days later she traveled to Boston to keep her speaking engagement.

Harriet made another trip down to Maryland that year. She brought out a couple and their two small children. But by now every road, North and South, carried a poster of Moses. The pro-slavers wanted her blood! Harriet's friends convinced her that now was the time to stop her trips. She was too important to the antislavery movement to get killed. She was far more useful alive.

Civil War

Harriet's days on the Underground Railroad were finished. But she was only forty years old. She wasn't ready for a rocking chair yet.

Over the years Harriet's speeches about her adventures as a conductor of the Underground Railroad were heard by many people. She never bragged of her great courage or her amazing ability to travel through the country undetected. But everyone who heard her speak was impressed by what she had done.

One of these people was the governor of Massachusetts, John Andrew. In 1861, when the Civil War broke out between the North and the South, he asked Harriet if she would work for the North.

Harriet agreed to help. In the spring of 1862 she traveled on the government transport ship *Atlantic* to an island off the coast of South Carolina. She was taken to the headquarters of General Isaac Stevens at Port Royal Island, where thousands of Northern soldiers were stationed. Thousands of Southern slaves were there, too.

At this time President Abraham Lincoln had not yet freed the slaves. But the war had forced many of their masters off the plantations. Some masters took their slaves away with them. Some shot their slaves rather than have them run off. But some slaves managed to escape. Many of them found their way to Port Royal.

Most of the male slaves wished to join the Northern army. They wanted to fight to help end slavery. But according to law, they were still slaves. They were not free to fight with the North.

At first things did not go well between the slaves and the Northern soldiers. The slaves knew only slavery. They expected the white Northern soldiers to act like their masters. They expected the soldiers to tell them what to do. The soldiers didn't know how to deal with the slaves. The soldiers and slaves had very different ways of speaking. When they tried to talk, they rarely understood each other.

Harriet's first job for the North was to assist the slaves. She acted as a go-between, helping them communicate with the soldiers. She encouraged them to make their own choices and to begin to think like free people. Harriet also taught black women how to make things that they could sell to the soldiers. She tried to help them find ways to earn their own living.

Harriet's next job for the North was that of a nurse. Many of her people nearly starved after they ran away from the life they knew on the plantations. Others caught terrible fevers and smallpox. But dysentery was the worst. It caused painful stomach cramps. Few who caught it survived.

Each morning Harriet went to the hospital. She sponged fevered brows, waved away flies, and bathed wounds. But each night more and more people died from dysentery.

Harriet started to wonder whether some of old Rit's herb medicines might help her patients. But she was hundreds of miles from Maryland, where the plants that she needed grew. Harriet decided to find out if they grew in South Carolina. In the woods she gathered the roots of white-flowering water lilies. She searched out an herb that looked like the beak of a bird. She boiled them together to make a dark, bitter mixture. She gave some of it to a man who was dying of dysentery. In a few days she could see that he was getting better. When nothing else helped, Harriet's medicine worked. Now a new legend sprang up about this remarkable woman. If Moses nursed you, you could not die.

Harriet traveled from camp to camp, offering her medicine and nursing skill to sick people. At night she returned to her own small cabin, where she baked pies and gingerbread and brewed rootbeer. She hired some of her people to sell these goods to the soldiers. In this way Harriet provided employment and made just enough money to live on.

At last, in 1863, Abraham Lincoln issued the Emancipation Proclamation, which freed the slaves in the Confederate States. Now the Southern black men could join the Northern Army. They formed their own all-black regiment, the First South Carolina Volunteers. No doubt Harriet felt proud and hopeful as she watched them parade down the street, escorted by a marching band of white soldiers. A thousand newly freed men were going off to fight against the people who once had owned them.

The Second South Carolina Volunteers was also a regiment made up of former slaves. Their commander was Colonel James Montgomery. He asked General Stevens if Harriet could be a scout for his troops. Both men knew that Harriet understood how to travel silently through swamp country. And she did not look dangerous. Colonel Montgomery wanted Harriet to go behind enemy lines. She could talk to blacks who were with their masters in the Confederate Army. They would trust her. They might even tell her about the movement of the Southern troops, their plans, and their hideouts. And so General Stevens appointed Harriet to her third job for the Union troops. Harriet became a spy.

In time Harriet became Commander of Intelligence Operations for the Union Army's Department of the South. She was in charge of a spy network that extended from South Carolina to the tip of Florida. She had river pilots and nine scouts under her command. These men weren't used to being led by a woman, least of all a black woman. But Harriet had earned an impressive reputation. She was famous for her courage. Just looking at her, soldiers could see her strength of character. No one grumbled about serving under Harriet Tubman.

In May of 1863 Harriet reported to General Stevens about her spy missions in the Combahee River area. The Combahee was a narrow river, running about fifty miles inland. Set back from its banks were huge plantations where food and supplies were stored for the Southern army. They were shipped to the soldiers by railroad, on tracks that ran alongside the Combahee and over its bridges. To protect their supplies, Southern soldiers planted mines in the river. If a boat went over a mine, it exploded like a bomb.

But Harriet knew rivers. She had spent hours wading in a freezing cold one to set Mr. Cook's muskrat traps. She had spent days cutting timber beside one for John Stewart. And she had waded through countless rivers to avoid capture on her many Underground Railroad journeys. Harriet and her scouts knew where every mine was planted on the Combahee. Harriet thought that Northern soldiers could get boats up the river without setting off the mines.

After he heard her report, General Stevens asked Harriet to join Colonel Montgomery in leading an invasion up the Combahee. Stevens ordered them to take about three hundred black soldiers with them. The object of the invasion was to knock out the railroad tracks and bridges. Then the Southern army would not be able to receive supplies. The soldiers were also to destroy or remove the river's mines. And, finally, they were to rescue as many slaves as they could.

Early on June 2, 1863, Harriet and the men started up the river in three gunboats. Harriet rode in the first, peering into the darkness. She and her scouts told the boat pilots where the mines were hidden. They very carefully removed them from the water.

Near a bend in the river Harriet ordered the pilot to slow down. She asked him to draw as near to the shore as he could. On the other side of the bend, Harriet knew that there was an enemy camp. Her troops quietly leapt from the gunboats and surrounded the camp. They captured it without firing a single bullet.

As the Northern gunboats came up the river, other Southern soldiers saw them and retreated. They tried to call for more soldiers to help them. But Harriet's men were quick. They jumped off their boats and raced to the plantations. There they set fire to enemy food supplies, their cotton, and their big houses.

Hundreds of slaves still worked on these plantations. When they saw the boats with black soldiers in them, they shouted, "Lincoln's gunboats have come to set us free!" They dropped whatever they were doing and ran for the river. Later Harriet recalled the hectic scene. "Sometimes the women would come with twins hanging round their necks; appears like I never seen so many twins in my life; bags on their shoulders, baskets on their heads, and young ones tagging behind, all loaded; pigs squealing, chickens screaming, young ones squalling."

Some black soldiers helped the escapees climb into rowboats. Then they rowed them to the gunboats. Other soldiers stayed on shore to keep the enemy occupied while the slaves got away.

At last the gunboats turned around and headed back east. When they finally reached their camp, Harriet discovered that 756 slaves had joined them. As in Harriet's other enterprises, not a single life of a slave or a Northern soldier was lost.

For the next several months Harriet continued to scout in enemy territory and to lead guerrilla expeditions for the North. She commanded troops with the authority of the best generals. She wore a pistol and wasn't afraid to use it. But Harriet also wore a long skirt, which made it awkward for her to run. In the days when Harriet had risked her life leading slaves to freedom, she disguised herself in men's clothing. But now she was a respected leader of the Northern forces. It would not be proper for her to dress in men's clothes. Yet she felt that wearing a skirt put her at a disadvantage in the field.

At about this time Harriet heard of a woman named Amelia Bloomer. Mrs. Bloomer was a pioneer for women's rights. She had designed what she called "a sensible costume for females." This was a small jacket with a short skirt worn over full trousers.

Harriet dictated a letter to a friend who, with a group of women, tried to see to it that Harriet got the things she needed for her work. Most of her clothes had been lost while being shipped to her. Harriet asked the woman if she could send her some new clothes. In the letter she said, "I want, among the rest, a bloomer dress, made of some coarse, strong material to wear on expeditions. In our late expedition up the Combahee River, in coming on board the boat, I was carrying two pigs for a poor sick woman, who had a child to carry, and the order 'double quick' was given, and I started to run, stepped on my dress, it being rather long, and fell and tore it almost off. . . . I made up my mind then I would never wear a long dress on another expedition of the kind, but would have a bloomer as soon as I could get it. So please make this known to the ladies, if you will, for I expect to have use for it very soon, probably before they can get it to me."

Harriet spied and fought for General Stevens for two years. By May of 1864 she was exhausted. She was also worried about her parents, so she decided to go home for a while. By this time the United States Government owed Harriet eighteen hundred dollars in back pay. While she was home, she began the long process of having friends write letters for her to help her get the money she was owed.

Back in Auburn, Harriet found that Ben

and Rit were doing as well as could be expected. In a short time Harriet felt rested and ready to go back to work. She traveled south again, this time to Washington, D.C. There she worked at the Fortress Monroe Hospital, nursing her people once more. Harriet was promoted to head nurse. In April of 1865 the war ended at last.

Harriet stayed and worked at the hospital for a few months after the war was over. Then she headed for home. As a nurse for the military, she was given a half-fare pass for riding trains.

She boarded a north-bound train and took a seat. When the conductor came by, she showed him her pass. But he only scowled.

"Come, hustle out of here!" he told her. "You can't sit here."

The conductor insulted her and said that her pass was no good because she was black.

Harriet patiently tried to explain that she had served in the army as a nurse. She was supposed to have a half-fare pass.

But the conductor didn't care. He grabbed her arm. Harriet resisted. Then the conductor called three more men to his side. None of the passengers riding in the train stood up to help Harriet. The four men threw her into the baggage car and shut the door. Bruised and bitter, she rode to New York inside the dark car.

When Harriet got off the train in Auburn, her friends were shocked by her appearance. Some thought she had been injured in the war.

"All those years of fighting, and never a scratch from a Rebel sword or gun," Harriet complained. "Had to wait till I was coming home to get my first war wound."

Years of Glory

In December of 1865 the Thirteenth Amendment to the Constitution was passed. It outlawed slavery in the United States. The battle Harriet fought for fifteen long years had been won. But Harriet learned on that train from Washington that it was still not an easy time for black people. Even though they were free now, black Americans didn't have the same rights as white Americans.

Harriet moved back into her old house on South Street in Auburn. Ben and Rit were quite old now, so Harriet looked after them. Other former slaves needed help, too. Some of them knocked on Harriet's door. Many of them were sick and poor. Harriet took them in and nursed them. She never turned anyone away.

To care for so many, Harriet needed the money the government owed her. Again, many

95

of her powerful friends, such as Frederick Douglass, wrote letters for her to send to Congress. A former slave like Harriet, Douglass was a leader of the antislavery movement before and during the war. He had spoken with President Lincoln about the problem of slavery, and he had received many awards and honors for his work. In a letter to Harriet which was sent on to the government, Douglass said:

Most that I have done and suffered in the service of our cause has been in public, and I have received much encouragement at every step of the way. You on the other hand have labored in a private way. . . . I have had the applause of the crowd and the satisfaction that comes of being approved by the multitude, while the most that you have done has been witnessed by a few trembling, scarred, and foot-sore bondmen and women, whom you have led out of the house of bondage, and whose heartfelt "God bless you" has been your only reward. The midnight sky and the silent stars have been the witnesses of your devotion to freedom and of your heroism.

But even this eloquent letter didn't help. The U.S. Government still didn't pay Harriet the money that it owed her.

Yet lack of money didn't stop Harriet from taking in people who needed her help. Among them was a soldier, Nelson Davis, whom Harriet had met when he was fighting in one of the black brigades for the North. Nelson, a big, good-looking man, was about twenty-eight years old. But he was sick with tuberculosis. He needed a place to stay. Although Rit grumbled about another mouth to feed, Harriet took Nelson in.

At last Harriet received money from an unexpected source. Sarah Bradford, a white woman, learned of Harriet's financial need and came up with an idea. She visited Auburn and listened to Harriet's stories for hours. In 1869 she published Harriet's biography, *Scenes in the Life of Harriet Tubman*. All the money that the book earned—twelve hundred dollars—went to Harriet.

Finally Harriet had enough money. She was sorry that it came too late to make Ben and Rit's last years more comfortable. They were dead by then, but both had lived to be well over ninety years old.

The same year Mrs. Bradford's book was published, in 1869, Harriet married Nelson Davis. He was about twenty years younger than

Harriet. Under her care he had gotten stronger. He was able to work as a brickmaker to help Harriet support her big "family."

Eventually the money from Mrs. Bradford's book ran out. But Harriet had many more stories to tell. So Sarah Bradford wrote another book, *Harriet Tubman: The Moses of Her People*.

Harriet hoped that the money from this second book would make a dream of hers come true. She wanted to found a home and hospital for people like the ones who came knocking on her door. Once again, Harriet tried to save her money.

To provide for her household she raised vegetables on her land. She peddled them from door to door. But she didn't just come with vegetables. She came with stories. At each house she was invited inside. Around the kitchen tables of Auburn, she sipped her favorite drink, hot tea with butter, while she told amazing tales of her days on the Underground Railroad.

In 1888 Nelson Davis died. Harriet received a pension of eight dollars a month as the widow of a soldier who had fought in the war. Later her pension was increased to twenty dollars a month. But her claim for the eighteen hundred dollars the government owed her was never settled.

To earn extra money Harriet still gave a lecture from time to time. She was frequently invited to speak by people who were trying to get the vote for women. Harriet was a good example of why women deserved equal rights with men. How many men had done the things she'd done?

At one meeting she spoke on the same platform as famous women's rights workers Susan B. Anthony and Elizabeth Cady Stanton. At the end of their speeches it was Harriet's turn. But Harriet had lapsed into one of her sleeping spells. Susan Anthony gently woke her and led Harriet to the speaker's platform.

"Ladies," she said, "I am glad to present you with Harriet Tubman, conductor of the Underground Railroad."

Harriet looked out at the audience. "Yes, ladies," she began, "I was the conductor of the Underground Railroad for eight years, and I can say what most conductors can't say. I never ran my train off the track and I never lost a passenger."

*　　*　　*

One day Harriet heard that the twenty-five acres across from her house were to be sold at auction. The property had two houses on it. They would be perfect for the home and hospital she had in mind. And the twenty-five acres was enough land for a small farm that could support the home.

With the little money she'd earned on the lecture platform and from her book money, Harriet set out for the auction. She knew that she didn't have enough money to afford the property. But Harriet had never stopped expecting miracles to happen.

When she came home from that auction, Harriet had a deed in her hand. A bank had loaned her the extra money she needed. Now it looked as if her dream for a home would come true.

Harriet moved her "family" into one of the two houses on the property and managed to scrape enough money together each month to pay the mortgage. As the 1800s came to a close, the house became a kind of shrine. Harriet herself was a legend. People read about her in Sarah Bradford's books. They wanted to meet her, to shake hands with this remarkable woman. People traveled great distances to see where the famous Harriet Tubman lived. She had interesting visitors from all over the world.

Harriet received many letters thanking her for the work she'd done. The mail carrier often read the letters aloud to her since she had never learned to read.

One day an unusual package came for Harriet. The mail carrier told her that it was from England. When she opened the package, she found two small boxes and a letter. The letter was signed "Victoria Regina." Harriet protested that she didn't know anyone with that name. Victoria Regina, the mail carrier explained, meant Queen Victoria. Harriet had received a letter from the queen of England!

When Queen Victoria read about Harriet's life, she wrote to congratulate Harriet on what she had done to help her people. The queen also invited her to London for her birthday celebration.

In one of the boxes Queen Victoria had sent Harriet a black silk shawl. In the other Harriet found a medal engraved with a picture of the queen and her family. It was a Diamond Jubilee Medal, celebrating sixty years of Victoria's reign.

But even letters from the queen of England did not ease Harriet's worries about money. At the age of eighty-two she was tired of coming up with the mortgage money each month. So in 1903 Harriet turned her house and land over to the African Methodist Episcopal Zion Church. She wanted her property to become a home for the poor, sick, and needy of her people. She still lived in the house, but it was managed by the church.

Harriet had taken strangers in for years. She never asked them for a penny. But the church committee didn't think it could run a home this way. They began to ask people who wanted to live in the home to pay a fee.

When she heard this, Harriet shook her head. "When I gave the home over to Zion Church, what do you suppose they did? Why, they made a rule that nobody should come in without a hundred dollars. Now I wanted to make a rule that nobody could come in unless they had no money. What's the good of a home if a person who wants to get in has to have money?"

Old and stooped, Harriet continued to take her walks along the streets of Auburn. At last her rheumatism got so bad that she needed a

wheelchair. Her grandnieces and grandnephews pushed her along the sidewalks. She rewarded them with tales of her days of adventure as "Moses" Tubman.

At the age of ninety-two Harriet became confined to her bed. But still she received many visitors. And someone read her the newspaper each day.

In the spring of her ninety-second year Harriet came down with pneumonia. She knew that she would not live much longer. She called her brother William Henry, who had lived with her since Nelson Davis had died, and some good friends to her bedside. With the help of two ministers they held a final service. Harriet led the singing:

Swing low, sweet chariot,
Comin' for to carry me home . . .

Harriet died on March 10, 1913. She was given a full military funeral. After she was gone, the city of Auburn, New York, missed their most famous citizen. They decided to do something to honor Harriet.

On June 12, 1914, all the flags in town were flown at half-mast. That night everyone gathered in the Auburn Auditorium. There were several speakers. One was Booker T. Washington. He, too, had been a slave. Like Harriet, he spent his life helping his people. He had founded the Tuskegee Institute, an outstanding school for blacks. Mr. Washington told how Harriet had "brought the two races nearer together" and "made it possible for the white race to place a higher estimate on the black race."

A bronze tablet was cast in Harriet's honor. It was placed on the front entrance of the Auburn Courthouse. The following words are among those engraved on the tablet:

IN MEMORY OF HARRIET TUBMAN.
BORN A SLAVE IN MARYLAND ABOUT
1821.
DIED IN AUBURN, N.Y., MARCH 10, 1913.
CALLED THE MOSES OF HER PEOPLE DUR-
ING THE CIVIL WAR.
WITH RARE COURAGE, SHE LED OVER
THREE HUNDRED
NEGROES UP FROM SLAVERY TO FREE-
DOM.

Harriet will always be remembered for her excellent "conducting" of the Underground Railroad. She never ran her train off the track. And she never lost a passenger.

Highlights in the Life of
HARRIET TUBMAN

1821   Slaves' births were not recorded, but it is believed Harriet was born this year.

1827   Harriet is first "hired out" by her master.

1834   Harriet helps a slave escape and receives a severe head injury as a result.

1844   Harriet marries John Tubman, a free man.

1849   Harriet escapes to freedom across the Mason-Dixon line.

1850   Harriet plans the successful escape of her sister Mary and family. The Fugitive Slave Law is passed. Now it is not safe for runaway slaves to live anywhere in America.

1851- Harriet becomes known as *Moses* and makes
1857   eleven trips to Maryland to lead slaves to freedom.

1854   Harriet leads three of her brothers and three other slaves to freedom.

1857   Harriet rescues her parents, Ben and Rit, and takes them to Canada.

1860   Harriet helps rescue fugitive slave Charles Nalle. She makes her nineteenth and last trip to Maryland to bring out slaves.

1862- Harriet becomes a nurse, scout, and spy for the
1863   Union forces during the Civil War.

106

1864   Harriet settles in Auburn, New York, to look after her parents.

1865   Harriet works in a hospital in Washington, D.C.

1869   *Scenes in the Life of Harriet Tubman* is published. Harriet marries Nelson Davis.

1886   *Harriet Tubman, the Moses of Her People* is published.

1913   On March 10, Harriet Tubman dies.

For Further Study

More Books to Read

Harriet Tubman. Judith Bentley (Franklin Watts)

Harriet Tubman. Jane Polcovar (Children's Press Choice)

Harriet Tubman. Marion Taylor (Chelsea House)

Harriet Tubman: Slavery and the Underground Railroad. Megan McClard (Silver Burdett)

Harriet Tubman: They Called Me Moses. Linda D. Meyer (Parenting Press)

Young Harriet Tubman: Freedom Fighter. Anne Benjamin (Troll Associates)

Videos

Harriet Tubman. (Schlessinger Video Productions)

Harriet Tubman and the Underground Railroad. (Phoenix/BFA Films & Video)

Harriet Tubman and the Underground Railroad. (CRM Films)

Index